Poor Poet's Psalter
Echoes of Psalms in Haiku
Musings to pray with

John E. Freal
2017

If you write poetry, it's your own fault.
    - Irish saying

Cover: This is a photographic collage with mirrors on the fundamental region of an apeirohedron, an unbounded or infinite polyhedron that divides three-dimensional space into two congruent regions. The fundamental region can generate the entire apeirohedron by translations in each of the three dimensions.

Poor Poet's Psalter
Echoes of Psalms in Haiku
Musings to Pray With

Copyright 2017 by John E. Freal. All rights reserved.
Portions - up to 25% - of the text may be quoted in any form without written permission.

Library of Congress Control Number: 2017932870

ISBN: 9780692841549

Introduction

I'm thankful for the experience of grace, the overwhelming presence of joy that I don't deserve but that sometimes comes in to my life. This feeling of grace can come at a family dinner, a gathering of friends, when I'm alone working on a piece of writing or shooting baskets in an empty gym, in church when a hymn or Christmas song catches me by surprise. It happened sometimes during my daily routine of prayer. That prayer usually includes the Psalms - I am thankful for the Psalms. Grace doesn't come because I pray the Psalms, but I wonder if I could recognize the grace that comes into my life if I didn't.

Several threads in my life had to come together to convince me to undertake a project like this. The most significant of these is that I have been reading, praying, editing, and living with the Psalms for over 40 years. In 1975, after making the decision to return to church, I asked our associate pastor, a young Catholic priest, about his daily spiritual practice. He said that he prayed the

Psalms, three each day. And when he finished the psalter, he started over again. That became my practice too. At least that was my practice for several years. I have missed days, months, and even over a year. I don't try to pray three Psalms at a time any more. Sometimes I just get lost in part of one Psalm, and sometimes I read five.

I've read the Psalms from a variety of Bible versions, the *Jerusalem Bible*, the *New Revised Standard Version*, the *New American Catholic Bible*, and Eugene Peterson's *The Message*. Norman Fischer is a poet who was raised Jewish and became a Zen Buddhist. He wrote versions of the Psalms in his own poetic language. For the past 14 years I've often been reading his versions of the Psalms which he titled *Opening to You*. Fischer didn't want to call God "Yahweh" or "Lord" or "He" or even "God." He thought "you" would be the most appropriate name for the God to whom the Psalms are addressed. In many Psalms the psalmists use that word too. I have found that it is also the most intimate way to pray, the way I understand God's presence in my prayers and in my life. The Psalms pushed my prayers in the direction of honesty and trust and thankfulness.

In addition to reading the Psalms, I found that I needed to do something else with them. I wrote verses from them in my journal. I have also calligraphed for myself my own versions of 18 of the Psalms, along with the Lord's Prayer and a few other verses of scripture. But these were mostly private. Early in my teaching career I was given a sky chart labeled "The Heavens." It immediately reminded me of Psalm 103, "As the heavens are high above the earth." So I put it on a wall of my classroom near the ceiling and got a map of the earth to put below it near the floor. During my years of teaching it reminded me daily of God's love for my students.

Another part of my morning routine has been journaling. But at the beginning of Lent in 2016 I felt that the journaling, rather than leading to prayer as had often happened, was getting in the way of it. So during Lent I went on a word fast, allowing myself to only write one or two words in my journal during my time of prayer and reflection. My experience was that that each word shone and often had a multiplicity of meaning. Some of the words were "gratitude," "cast about," "divinity/dignity," "courage/freedom," and "vulnerable."

So there were four strands that came together that made me want to do something new with the Psalms.

First, I wanted to make words shine, have multiple meanings, and have relationships like chords in music.
Second, I wanted to go through all the Psalms again which I had not done in a longtime.
Third, I wanted to put on Facebook something that wasn't a selfie.
And fourth, I discovered haiku, a Japanese poetic form with a 5 syllable line, a 7 syllable line, and another 5 syllable line. 17 syllables all together with the purpose of expressing an idea. I would describe it as a way to invent new thought-words or perhaps a way to put words together like chords in music. After finishing these haiku, I discovered that musical chords might be an appropriate metaphor as haiku are supposed to connect different even clashing ideas within the poem and make reference to something outside it.

So I tried to make a haiku on what had been a daily prayer, some verses from Psalm 90.

Your light - your beauty
Make known how you live in me
Bless all my children

I wrote a few more haiku in late May but put haiku aside because I was finishing another writing project. In late June a haiku for Psalm 1 came to me.

Give fruit in season
Delight in loveliness
Remembered by God

I wrote in my journal that it felt wonderful to do this - possibly it will be wonderful to someone else.

Psalm 2 was at first difficult for me.

We try to run from
The kingdom of being to
Find another home

"Jarring," I wrote in my journal, "but appropriately so; it seems to be what Psalm 2 says."

By June 30, in 2016 I had written haiku for the first eight Psalms. Then this next haiku, a kind of Psalm 0, was put on Facebook on July 1st to introduce what I was going to do.

The Psalms in haiku
One each day as Time permits
Aiming for essence

The Psalms are divided into 5 books. I have kept this structure which dates from Hebrew times, and have given my own title to each of the books. The first is called *Fault Lines* because these lines are my fault. *Fault Lines* also carries a memory of my ancient ancestor, St. Columcille (or Columba as it was Latinized), founder of many monasteries in Ireland and Scotland, as well as the patron saint of poets. Columcille got this designation for defending poets, who were often pagan bards, against the Irish nobles and the Irish church even though poets were sometimes at fault when poking fun at church and political leadership. While I have not made fun of the psalmists, many times I have disagreed with or have been unable to express honestly some of their sentiments, especially when they want God to crush enemies. Sometimes I ignore their themes, and a few times even change them. Fortunately there's almost always something in each psalm for me to affirm. For this I gladly accept fault.

Book 2 of these Haiku Psalms is called *Honesty and Trust*. The Psalms in their very nature are prayers of honesty. We can't live with them for very long without being honest with God. Similarly, the Psalms are prayers of trust in God's love. Trust might be another way of saying faith though not a faith in specific doctrines but faith in our relationship with God. There's nothing necessarily wrong with doctrines, but these doctrines can limit us to only cognitive understandings, that is, ways that we can talk to each other about God. In Psalm 50 the psalmist, Asaph, has God speak about trust and relationship.

> Offer me your heart's intention
> Pay me your forged words
> Give me your sorrows - call on me
> So I can answer you
> So that your soul can speak to me
>
> From Norman Fischer's *Opening to You*

I tried to name the five books using a common theme in many, though certainly not all, of the Psalms they contained. Anne Lamont has defined the 3 types of prayer as help, thank you, and wow. Since many of these Psalms in Book 3 involved asking for help in the presence of eminent danger, it seemed *Running for Cover* was a good title.

Book 4 contains my two favorite Psalms. Psalm 90 is the only one called a Psalm of Moses, and brings many Old Testament themes together. Psalm 103 is for me David's best work, his Psalm about God's love. More than any other this Psalm opens my heart, hence the title, *Open Hearts*.

I learned from Eugene Peterson that many of the Psalms in Book 5 are songs of pilgrimage, especially Psalms 120-134, so the title of Book 5 is *Songs Along the Way*. The pilgrimage metaphor may be helpful to bring to all our prayers.

On July 2, 2016, my mother would have been 101. She died 3 years ago and her memory is still very much with me. I posted the haiku for Psalm 1 on her birthday in part to honor her inspiration throughout my life. I posted haiku for Psalm 150, the last psalm, on December 2. That would have been my father's 99th birthday. The ending date wasn't intentional until a few weeks before when I realized that the postings would be done sometime around then. My father passed away over 40 years ago. But only recently have I begun to see his loves, joys, sorrows, talents, sacrifices, burdens, his care for his children, and his love for our mother. I have often wished that I could have made peace with him before he died. Through the process of writing some of my prayers this way I have made peace with his memory, a kind of healing - or possibly made peace with him if you believe in the communion of saints. The process of writing these haiku has perhaps changed me in other ways that I don't yet understand.

There is extra space between the haiku for you to write or draw or doodle as you read through them. My hope is that you might be opened to or affirmed in the beauty of prayer.

Haiku with an asterix have additional information in the Notes section at the end of the book.

The figure with five-fold symmetry at the beginning of each section is a wave function in polar form.

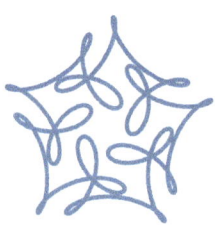

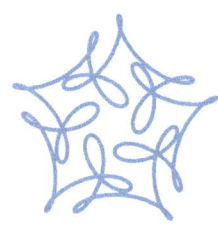

Book 1 - Fault Lines - Psalms 1-41

1
Give fruit in season
Delight in the loveliness
Remembered by God

2
We try to run from
The kingdom of being to
Find another home

3
My foes surround me
But you bless me anyway
I can live with that

4
Offer your stillness
Trust the rightness of being
Receive heaven's light

5
Encircling kindness
Bids us enter your presence
Bless us - we're open

6
Have mercy on us
For we are fading away
Only love saves us

7
Let the enemy
Draw his sword and make ready
Instruments of death

8*

8
We are very small
And yet you remember us
Giving us your light

9
You rebuke nations
You hear the cry of the poor
Our hope in trial

10
Ambush and deceit
Lurking near the villages
Have you forgotten

11
A shot in the dark
Shakes our foundations until
You give us refuge

12
Honesty is gone
Our language only makes lies
Your word keeps us whole

13
Did you forget me
Look here - answer when I call
I trust your kindness

14
Fools cannot trust you
Only those with nothing left
Come to you in hope

15
Who dwells with I am
Who speaks the truth from the heart
In hard times keeps faith

16
Not requirements
You are my share and my cup
Your word is my joy

17
We call upon you
Test us and find no evil
Let us know your love

18
Enclosed by darkness
Then rescued by your kindness
Cause our lights to shine

19-1
Their voice falls silent
Your music plays everywhere
Speaking your beauty

19-2
Preserve us from pride
Help us always hear your word
Speak joy to our hearts

20
We trust in your grace
Acting in your world may our
Partials become whole

21
You crown us with strength
Steadfast love will keep us whole
Evil will not win

22-1*
You abandoned us
Prisoners of the lie that
Work shall make us free

22-2*

22-3*
Life is suffering
You have been here all along
We live in your heart

23-1*

23
I am content now
You lead to the path of truth
My cup overflows

23-2
Light in the darkness
Preparing parties for friends
Forever with us

24
Clean hands and pure hearts
Your glory beyond our dreams
Do we know you yet

25
We have much to learn
Teach us the way we should grow
Blessed by your friendship

26
We are innocent
Your beauty is our haven
Test our hearts in fire

27
Your presence is hope
You are my light and rescue
Even in the dark

28
In you my heart trusts
Thanksgiving becomes my song
Singing my delight

29
Wind can break cedars
The call shakes all foundations
Your voice blesses us

30
The pit of despair
Held me until your morning
Turned fear to dancing

31
We are in distress
Let us not be put to shame
Your kindness calms us

32
You teach us the way
If we are honest with you
Forgiveness is ours

33
Not saved by armed might
Your presence provides defense
We trust your I am

34
They cry out - you hear
You are close to the broken
Bringing them back home

35
Chaff before the wind
At my stumbling they gathered
Evil for goodness

36
O fountain of life
All people may take refuge
In your steadfast love

37
Like smoke they vanish
Oppressors of the lowly
When justice comes forth

38
No health in my bones
My heart throbs and is broken
I ask for healing

39-1
Let me know my end
We stand as only a breath
Our hope is in you

39-2
I will be silent
What is dear to me is gone
My life a mere breath

40-1
Sacrifice is past
Your law is deep in our hearts
Your love is our guide

40-2
We wait patiently
And your faithfulness keeps us
In the stream of love

41
Confessing my faults
May I praise you in the end
Amen and amen

May the Trinity
Always live in you and you
In the Trinity

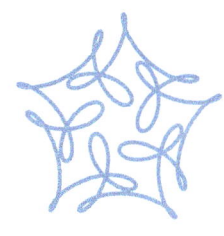

Book 2 - Honesty and Trust - Psalms 42-72

42-1
Why am I downcast
One day I will give you thanks
When wholeness is mine

42-2
The others tease me
Where is your I am - show us
My heart is broken

43*

43
Sighing I wander
Till your truth and light lead to
Your holy mountain

44
Scorn of our neighbors
Do not turn your face away
Shadow dark as death

45
Not limits but you
We open to your wonder
And stand anointed

46
Be still and know me
I am what humans hope for
Come - behold my works

47-1
Let our music play
Forever in praise of you
Queen of all the earth

47-2
Let our music play
Forever in praise of you
King of all the earth

48
Tell all our children
We ponder your steadfast love
*Ora pro nobis**

49
Sheol is our home
Unless God ransoms our souls
Death makes us equal

50
I am rescues you
When you call in troubled times
Bring a heart of thanks

51
Against you we sinned
Create in us hearts of truth
Give us joy again

52
They change white for black
And love malicious gossip
We will stay faithful

53
Turning life around
We forget to simply live
Forget to call you

54
Outlaws out to kill
Rescue me from these troubles
You helped me before

55
Friends betray - break trust
Knowing you will make me whole
Shelter from the storm

56*

56
Enemies attack
I will praise you anyway
You collect my tears

57
Take pity on us
Dawn is the hour of rescue
You save the oppressed

58
Corruption comes in
The reward for the people
Is to see it out

59
Lies he says to us
Let him be caught in his pride
You are our fortress

60
Your people suffer
We wonder what can be next
Our defense is broken

61
On the outside still
Bring me home to your mountain
Singing your blessings

62-1
We are but a breath
Yet we have your steadfast love
Silently we wait

62-2
Once you spoke to us
Strength love and justice are yours
Twice we heard your words

63*

63
We are wandering
In a dry and weary land
Drinking in your strength

64
Their tongues are like swords
Bitter words are their arrows
Their lies undo them

65
Hope of all people
You guide the waters of life
Your bounty is ours

66
The whole earth gives thanks
You brought us to a good place
Through fire and ice

67
We will praise the light
Let your way be known to all
Be gracious to us

68
Foes vanish like smoke
You give the lonely a home
Captives get freedom

69
There is no foothold
The waters have come up high
You know my folly

70
Please deliver me
Let the shameful be confused
I need your help now

71
You are my fortress
Rescue me from the unjust
When my strength is spent

72
When the poor call you
Let the people see justice
Like rain on the earth

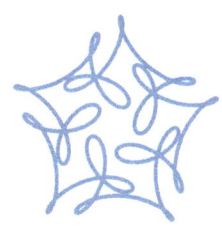# Book 3 - Running for Cover - Psalms 73-89

73
Envy is foolish
The arrogant meet their end
Swept out by terrors

74
Have you cast us off
Give us reason to praise you
When these foes speak lies

75
To the proud - let go
And to bullies - not so fast
I am will be judge

76
War weapons broken
You inspire fear in the kings
Praise to you alone

77*

77
Is our time ended
Or will we see your power
A way through the sea

78
You helped us often
And many times we complained
Help us be faithful

79
Holy place destroyed
Our dead not even buried
Rescue and forgive

80
We have tears to drink
Our enemies laugh at us
Turn again O God

81-1
Listen to Me now
Come out from your narrowness
Keep your soul's beauty

81-2
If you had heard Me
All the world would bend to good
Sweetness flow from rocks

82
Wickedness prospers
Give justice to the lowly
All are her children

83
Like chaff in the wind
As fire burns a forest
Unless we seek you

84
Our home in beauty
Knowing you listen to us
We pray - dream - sing here

85
Give us life again
Peace and justice will embrace
Your glory with us

86
The insolent rise up
Unaware of your great love
Your servants trust you

87*

87
Happy those born here
May we be borne here again
Captured by your love

88
My cares are heavy
You've driven my friends away
Nothing more to lose

89
We doubt your presence
As events wash over us
How long can we last

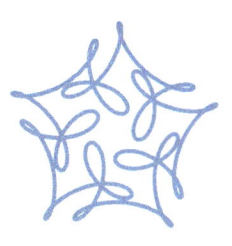

Book 4 - Open Hearts - Psalms 90-106

90-1
Your light - your beauty
Make known how you live in me
Bless all my children

90-2
Our time is fleeting
Teach us to number our days
With hearts of wisdom

91
Elyon* rescues us
We need not fear life's terrors
I am - our refuge

92*

92
Grow like a cedar
Still producing in old age
Always green and full

93*

93
Your goodness finds us
Beyond the thunder of waves
Past the end of time

94
Widow and stranger
Are sacrificed by these fools
O God be our help

95*

95 Who formed depths and heights
Help us listen to your voice
Let us sing to you

96
I am brings justice
Seas thunder and heavens sing
The whole earth is glad

97
Idols are worthless
The triumph of I am is
Joy for honest hearts

98
Nature rejoices
You come to judge the nations
And tribes with justice

99
Our heroes called you
You answered them from a cloud
Forgiving their sins

100
Our praise has a ground
Your love endures forever
Faithfulness through time

101
There are no small sins
Slander - arrogance - deceit
Help me find the way

102-1
Give me a hearing
My days pass away like smoke
Comfort my children

102-2
Marching to death's door
Seeing my life in the dust
Still I will praise you

103-1
As high as heaven
Above the earth - so great is
Your kindness to us

103-2
Forgiving our sins
You awaken the spirit
So time is refreshed

103-3
My soul remembers
A blessing for your I am
All that is within

103-4
Generosity
Is blind to our shortcomings
Your gifts are gracious

103-5*

103-6
Embracing us all
Blessings to you from angels
Who carry your word

103-7
Your love stretches from
Forever to forever
Flows to our children

104
All are created
Through the Spirit - you renew
The face of the earth

105
We sing praise to you -
Remember your faithfulness
Opening the rock

106
We have been reckless
Worshipping our golden calves
Wounding our children

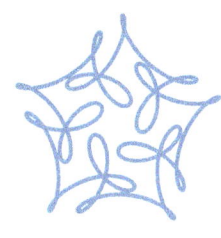

Book 5 - Songs Along the Way - Psalms 107-150

107
Distressed in the boat
From the storm you rescued us
Waves of the sea hushed

108
Help against the foe
So that we may be rescued
And praise you again

109
They trade blame for love
My heart is pierced within me
My friends betray me

110
You will be tested -
Be refreshed along the way
Know God is with you

111
Holy is your name
Your presence brings wisdom
Your praise brings us light

112
Blessed by your presence
We can be generous and
A light in darkness

113
Praise you forever
From the dust you raise the poor
To put them with kings

114
The sea rolls away
The earth trembles - I am comes
Rocks become fountains

115
Their feet cannot walk
Blind deaf mute are their idols
They will be like them

116
I shall take the cup
To give thanks for your great love
For hearing my call

117
Praise - Alleluia
All people will know your love
Faith never ending

118
Let each one witness
And let every house proclaim
Love is forever

119
Turn my heart to you
Open my eyes to your life
Your word is my light

120
Woe to this stranger
The path they seem to want is
War instead of peace

121
My help comes from you
Maker of heaven and earth
You make my steps safe

122
We will seek your good
We will say - peace be with you
O Jerusalem*

123
Enough opinions
Too much distain from the rich
Our souls need mercy

124
We would have been drowned
If you had not been with us
You have kept us whole

125
You encircle us
On paths leading to goodness
Not so the crooked

126
We left in chaos
Returned to our homes singing
With a great harvest

127
Our children are gifts
Unless I am builds with us
We labor in vain

128
Give us food to eat
Help us to walk in your ways
Families at peace

129
When we lose our way
We become our enemies
Our blessings wither

130
Forgiveness for us
Hope for all to find wholeness
My soul waits for you

131
Now my heart is calm
I am content with my lot
Trusting in I am

132
We won't return home
Can't even rest till we find
The place where you are

133
Life forevermore
Together in unity
Your blessing for us

134
At night we bless you
In holy places find you
Find our redemption

135
Perhaps it will be
That they become like the gods
Whom they have worshipped

136
Presence in our time
Your love endures forever
Thank you for these gifts

137-1
We sat down and wept
In this strange land of exile
We remembered home

137-2
Vengeful violence
Would make me ever so glad
Done to them and theirs

138
I walk through troubles
And remember to give thanks
Your hand preserves me

139-1
As darkness has light
You search me and know my heart
Lead me in your way

139-2
I was in your plan
And you put me together
Formed me as I am

139-3
Your infinities
Are around us to explore
We are still with you

140
Your justice guides us
Protect us from violence
Attacks along the way

141
I just might be wrong
Let the truthful correct me
But don't turn my heart

142
No refuge remains
You can save me from darkness
Give heed to my cry

143
My heart is heavy
Teach me the way I should go
Let your spirit lead

144
We are but a breath
And our days like a shadow
Yet your blessings come

145
May your works bless you
Of grace and steadfast love
Our children will know

146
You made land and sea
Your justice lifts the lowly
My soul will praise you

147
You care for Zion*
Heal the brokenhearted
Put songs in our hearts

148
Praise from your angels
Earth air fire and water
Praise from young and old

149
Rejoice with dancing
Sing to I am a new song
Let your faith be praise

150
We praise in your house
Trust you under open skies
Now let all praise you

From Richard Rohr's 2013 essay on Silence
Grace comes from nowhere
Our faith needs to trust silence
So simple and clear

Remembering T.S. Eliot
End is beginning
Our time may move in other
Possibilities

Matthew 6:9-13
Close as air we breathe
Give and forgive and keep us
In the stream of love

Joshua 1:9
Be strong - have courage
Neither frightened nor dismayed
I am is with you

On the passing of Mary Lou - my mother-in-law
Morning brings mourning
She prayed all goodness for us
We are orphans now

From a letter of Dostoyevsky at age 16
One sees with the heart
Nature - the soul - God's love
And not through reason

Notes

Whatever haiku communicate should be nearly immediate, a process Malcolm Gladwell describes in *Blink*. We feel this immediacy when we recognize a face or hear a favorite song. Even so, I don't claim any of that immediacy with this collection. You will have to evaluate that for yourself. However, the haiku for Psalms 22 and 23 need some background because they were so personal compared to all the others. Notes for some of the photographs are also provided as well as notes about words that might be unfamiliar.

22
Psalm 22 begins with a dark lament, echoed, in part, by Jesus from the cross (Mark 15:34), but in verse 23 this Psalm turns into a hymn of praise. The Psalm says that even in the face of suffering and death we can praise God. Initially I could find no single haiku that would do this. (You might try reading one of the haiku from Psalm 102 followed by one from 103 to understand what I failed to achieve in the first two haiku for Psalm 22. Or

even better, listen to Beethoven's Fifth Symphony, paying close attention to the transition from the third to the fourth movements.) So my first haiku for Psalm 22 stayed with only the dark lament. My own visual image for Haiku 22-1 was the gate of the Dachau concentration camp inscribed with the words, "Arbeit macht frei." "Work makes you free," is a lie in the historical sense that the Nazis never intended to free the prisoners from the camps. It might be a lie in the theological/philosophical sense too in that our works don't make us free either. I was looking online for just the right image of the Dachau gate on which to write Haiku 22-1. I never did find one, but what I find instead led to Haiku 22-2.

Online I found a picture of my father and his sergeant viewing a pile of dead bodies a day or two after liberation of the Dachau camp in the spring of 1945. When snooping through my father's things as a teen, I had seen an album of similar pictures. The pictures may have been used as exhibits during the Nuremberg Trials where my father also was assigned. My mother had told me that at the end of the war my father was adjutant to General

Patton, commander of the American Third Army. Because Patton was sick when the photographers arrived to document the atrocities of the Dachau camp, my father was assigned to take them around and tell them what to photograph. I don't think my father authorized himself to be in any of the photos. The picture was taken without his knowledge. But there he is in profile, quite literally confronting the problem of evil. At the end of the war my father stayed on near Dachau for some days or even weeks helping to care for survivors. Later that summer he wanted his wife to come to Europe to be with him while he stayed on Patton's staff to help set up facilities for the War Crime Trials in Nuremberg. The army was willing but my mother was not. My father stayed in Europe until the end of 1945 and then came home.

I was very surprised to find this photo. After my father died in 1975, I looked from time to time in my mother's storage places for the photos I had seen as a teen. I looked for 30 years. In 2006, my mother finally admitted that she had burned the album of Dachau photos that my father had kept since the war. She did this in 1975 right after his death. I remembered coming into the house to help her move and thinking it was unusual to have a fire on moving day during the summer. For having the feelings she did about the Dachau photos and for burning them, I don't blame her.

23

The photo used with this haiku was taken in the Japanese Garden in Seattle, and it is only in part included because of cultural ties between haiku and Japanese gardens. The Japanese Garden in the University of Washington's Arboretum is a place where I would often go with my daughter when she was young. But on the dark, rainy day when this photo was taken, Emily had just undergone brain surgery. Even though the two haiku for Psalm 23 remind us of God's presence, the photo can tell us that the valley of the shadow of death is there too.

8

Night sky - no source found

43

Photograph of a print of a 19th century Japanese painting of Mt. Fuji.

48

"Ora pro nobis" means "pray for us." This Latin response was often used in Christian litanies.

56

Stations of the Cross at the Passion entrance of the Basilica of the Holy Family - Sagrada Familia - in Barcelona, Spain

63 and 77

Photographs of prints given to my mother by abstract expressionist Matsumi Kanemitsu (1922-1992)

87

Winterscape, looking across Drayton Harbor in Blaine, Washington

91

"Elyon" means "The Most High" in Hebrew. The psalm has four names for God in the first strophe. Two other strophes speak of angels.

92

The tree is not a cedar but a Utah juniper, a member of the same biological family as the varieties of cedar.

93

Pacific Ocean near Newport, Oregon

95

Grand Canyon, Arizona

103-5

Photograph of a poster advertising an exhibition of *The Saint John Bible* at the Minneapolis Institute of Arts in 2005

122

Jeru > founded of God

shalam > to be safe, to be completed, by extension to be friendly, to make full, to be at peace

147

Zion is the Hebrew name for the Temple Mount in Jerusalem, a holy place.

www.ingramcontent.com/pod-product-compliance
Lightning Source LLC
Chambersburg PA
CBHW051540010526
44107CB00064B/2795